———————— Royal Jel

The new guide to nature's richest health food

——Royal Jelly——

The new guide to nature's richest health food

Irene Stein

THORSONS PUBLISHING GROUP

First published 1989

British Library Cataloguing in Publication Data

Stein, Irene
Royal jelly - the new guide to nature's richest health food.
1. Man. Health. Improvement. Use of royal jelly
I. Title
613.2' 6

ISBN 0-7225-2159-6

*Published by Thorsons Publishers Limited, Wellingborough,
Northamptonshire NN8 2RQ, England*

Typeset by Burns & Smith, Derby
Printed in Great Britain by Mackays of Chatham, Kent.

1 3 5 7 9 10 8 6 4 2

Contents

──Acknowledgements──

My thanks go to the many people who have helped me in writing this book: to Susan Merriman and Judy Quin, who helped to give my words their full meaning; to Ann and her team for their work on the book; to Keith and Gerry, trusted friends, for all their support; to Bob Ledger for his sensitive drawings; to Stephen Hampshire for his photographic work; to the Chinese, for providing the best royal jelly in the world; and to everyone at Regina.

I am, of course, particularly grateful to royal jelly itself, for providing the energy I needed to achieve all I have achieved. Especial thanks go to my family: to Jane and Lisa for allowing me space to do everything I've done; to Jack and Sophie for providing me with the opportunity to be determined and to stick by what I believe in; and to Sophie in particular for being a shining example of the benefits of royal jelly after taking it for 15 years.

Then I should like to thank the team currently doing research into the medical evidence for royal jelly's powers. Finally, I should like to thank Brad Brown for enabling the team to grow in harmony.

——— Foreword ———

With few exceptions most useful discoveries are dependent upon a pioneer, or innovator, who stands in the face of suspicions and oppositions in order to make clear the benefits of a discovery or new product. Without such 'pioneers' we would still be earthbound and pulling carts and wagons with animals. We'd very likely be taking drinking water from the polluted Thames river, and filling our bodies with sugar, saturated fats, red meat and carcinogens, thinking it is healthy for us because it tastes good.

Irene Stein is one of those pioneers in the western world. Her discovery of royal jelly, the benefits of which have been well known in the east for centuries, especially China, has placed her in the unique position of being an advocate for a product which is new to our way of thinking. It assaults our preconceived western judgements to think that anything can be quite this good. I recall my own introduction to royal jelly by Irene. When I complained of symptoms of chronic fatigue, she said royal jelly could help. With tongue in cheek I humoured her and took the fresh royal jelly she provided. Within a few weeks I was feeling more healthy and vibrant. Other symptoms cleared up as well. Still, I was reluctant to credit the product she recommended. But Irene is a pioneer and with 'true grit' she has persevered with people like myself to make the value of royal jelly known to a broad population. Today she is a leading authority on this product.

People who make a difference in the world are often motivated by a vision of service to mankind: this is certainly true of the author of this book. Irene has been committed to her own health and well-being for much of her adult life. She has been willing to push out the parameters of her own thinking about health to include the wisdom and knowledge of other cultures and to use this knowledge to nurture her own healthy body and pass it on to others. She practises what she preaches, and the advantages, particularly of using royal jelly, appear to be significant. In this way she is able, with personal authority, to support others to receive salutary benefits as well. Because she has persisted for several years to advocate royal jelly as an important product for healing many health problems, her mail is filled with thousands of appreciative comments and testimonials from people she set out to serve with her insights and knowledge of this natural product.

It is very difficult to say what impact royal jelly has had on Irene's attitude or motivation. However, those who know her, as I do, recognize her to be a woman of unique and consistent sensitivity to people. She has an unswerving commitment to lead her company to become a healthy organization which is dedicated to the well-being of its employees, while offering the public a product of significant and lasting value.

Today Irene is not alone. She has a large staff and a group of supporters who are seriously studying the reasons why royal jelly is such a rich addition to western health aids, and who are considering the further implications of its use in the future. She is no longer the lone pioneer I met several years ago trying to get a few of us to try it out, but a leading spokesperson and for a growing and more educated public. We can guess with some degree of assurance that within a few years we will see another book from her about royal jelly that will further enhance our knowledge about this amazing product that comes from the world of nature and enters our world to improve our health and well-being.

K. Bradford Brown Ph.D.

──────Introduction──────

When, three years ago, I put down my pen after finishing the last sentence of the last chapter of *Royal Jelly: A guide to nature's richest health food* (published by Thorsons), I realized that I had touched only the tip of the iceberg. Even as the book went to press, I learned about new research and novel applications for this wonderful substance. Over the months I have been delving even deeper into the subject, collating all the information I uncovered: now I feel the time is ripe for a new volume.

The truth is that I am continually intrigued and amazed by new facts which come to light about this product of the hive. There seems to be no limit to the range of products in which royal jelly can be used, no end to the beneficial effects which can be derived from this miraculous substance. Yet one mystery remains. Scientists have accounted for 96 per cent of the ingredients of royal jelly but, despite intensive research, the nature of that last 4 per cent remains tantalizingly elusive.

It is now some 15 years since I first started my own royal jelly regime of one 150 mg capsule per day, taken first thing in the morning with a glass of water. At that time I was plagued by ill health and was living on diuretics, which were sapping my energy far more than the excess water. One of the first benefits I discovered of taking royal jelly was its natural diuretic action — I could soon throw those pills away! The effect on my general level of well-being, stamina and youthfulness has continued to be felt over the years. Niggling ailments which seemed to lurk round every corner miraculously disappeared. I took a major gynaecological operation in my stride with the minimum interruption of my busy business schedule. Also, I have achieved and maintained a level of energy and a workrate which would be remarkable even in a 20-year-old, and my 50th birthday looms large on the horizon! In fact, although my business and workload have grown steadily over the years, the cumulative benefits of taking royal jelly have more than kept pace.

Of course, once I realized to what extent royal jelly was

improving my quality of life I spread the word to all and sundry, especially my own family. My mother, Sophie, is an inspiration to me and to everyone who knows her. Although she is now looking forward to her eighties, she is as bright and energetic as a woman half her age. When I first introduced her to my discovery, she was a long-time arthritic. After taking royal jelly for only a short time, her crippling pain began to diminish until, at length, it disappeared completely. Thankfully, the condition has not reared its ugly head since.

Even my two daughters thrive on royal jelly. Lisa, in particular, was very susceptible in her early years to any infectious disease which was going the rounds, from the common cold to the usual litany of childhood illnesses, and when she caught them she really suffered. This was where one of royal jelly's key benefits came up trumps. Her general health and resistance to infection received a major boost and she changed from being a frequent absentee to having an excellent record of attendance at school. As an added bonus, the royal jelly cleared up her eczema. In Lisa's teenage years, the royal jelly regime helped her to sail through her 'A' level exams and is today proving to be a valuable aid in her degree studies.

My daughter Jane derived similar benefits from taking royal jelly during her childhood. Her days of having one cold after another are now long gone. There was one thing Jane *did* catch while she was still a child, however, and that was my enthusiasm for royal jelly! Now she is a vivacious, lovely young woman, working alongside me to spread the royal jelly story, to the beauty salon world in particular.

There are many benefits to be derived from using a natural substance, as the herbalists among you will know. Indeed, the West as a whole is slowly but surely moving towards a natural approach to health improvement and maintenance. To my mind, where royal jelly is concerned, three of the principal benefits of taking it are that, in contrast to what one might call 'synthetic' remedies, there is not the slightest risk of addiction, it is non-allergenic, and the body never becomes immune to its effects.

I heartily wish that the same could be said for modern medicines. When I read about the traumas experienced by those who suffer from tranquillizer addiction, about patients having to be given increasingly large doses of analgesics as their bodies become resistant to the pain-killing effects of the medications — and, come to that, when I read about youngsters experimenting with illegal drugs in an attempt to put some sparkle into their lives, it is then above all that I really appreciate the value of what Mother Nature has provided for a mental and physical 'lift'.

It has been estimated that up to a third of hospital patients are admitted suffering from the effects of modern medicine. I am not by any means condemning conventional treatments out of hand, but I do feel that prevention of disease is so much better than any cure, and that more emphasis should be placed on the holistic approach to medicine — seeing the person as a whole, rather than treating isolated symptoms.

That being said, taking royal jelly is only part of my recipe for a healthy and happy life. Naturally, I do not smoke, although I have great sympathy for those who are having problems in kicking the habit. However, I do have the occasional alcoholic drink, but I *do* mean 'occasional'! I know my body's reactions very well and I am sensitive to its adverse reaction to even a so-called 'normal' intake of alcohol.

I am a great believer in fresh air and exercise. These days the only time many people have a breath of fresh air or exercise is when they walk the few yards from their house to their car in the morning, from the car park to the office, and the same again when they go home in the evening. Fresh air is so invigorating! I go for a brisk three- or four-mile walk every morning for the exercise, to clear out my lungs, and to clear my mind and thought processes. It works absolute wonders! On the same subject, I am a fervent believer in the benefits of doing yoga breathing exercises, thereby making the best of each breath of air while at the same time relieving tension and improving muscle tone.

When it comes to skin care products, everything I put on my face contains royal jelly, and that includes tonic and moisturizer, as well as royal jelly & vitamin E cream for any blemishes. My skin is therefore in good condition, and I wear lipstick and eye make-up to feel my best. This royal jelly skin care range has only recently come onto the market, but already it is proving extremely popular. I must say that I also owe the good condition of my hair to royal jelly. But, for an even more impressive example of hair which not only retains its look and strength but also its colour, I must again cite the example of Sophie, my mother.

Yes, it is astonishing to think that royal jelly has such remarkable effects, and in the following pages you will find many accounts of even more remarkable improvements in health and general well-being not only in people, but also in animals. Also included in my book are many amazing facts which have come to light during my research into the scientific work which has been done on royal jelly in recent years.

Even after all this time, I am still occasionally surprised at the wide range of its applications. Only a few weeks ago, I was on holiday in Israel when I cut my foot on a piece of coral while swimming in the sea. The wound was deep and bled profusely — I even wondered whether I should not have it stitched up. It was so pain-

ful that I could not even stand but, before resorting to calling in a
doctor, I decided to try some natural remedies. I applied aloe vera
juice, with no effect, so, that night, I cut open a fresh royal jelly
capsule and applied the contents to the wound. I repeated the ap-
plication on the two following nights and, to my delight and relief,
the cut healed up like magic.

I am not alone in my enthusiasm for this wonderful product of
the hive: the number of people who have made this marvellous
substance part of their lives is growing all the time. If you are not
yet a member of the worldwide royal jelly fraternity, I hope that by
the time you have finished reading my book you will be.

Some people wonder whether the effect it has on them may be
psychological rather than physical. I am not one of them. Far from
it, because I have seen too much evidence to the contrary. For
example, impressive results have been achieved by giving animals
royal jelly and in such cases any 'placebo' effect can be discounted.

The fact is that, however sceptical you may be, it is impossible to
ignore the *physical* changes in people who take royal jelly. One of
my correspondents had been suffering from septicaemia and began
to take royal jelly capsules. When she attended for her three-
monthly check-up, her doctor simply said, 'I don't care what you
are taking, just keep taking it. Your blood is so much improved it is
now better than mine!' Need I say more?

April 1989

CHAPTER 1

_ How doth the little busy _ bee...

Bees have fascinated man since time immemorial; indeed more has been written about bees than about any other animal — except man. Literature is littered with references to bees, from Virgil, who wrote of them in his *Georgics*, to Shakespeare's 'Where the bee sucks, there suck I' and Tennyson's 'murmuring of innumerable bees' not forgetting, of course, Isaac Watts' poem entitled, 'Against Idleness and Mischief' (later to be parodied wickedly by Lewis Carroll):

How doth the little busy bee
Improve each shining hour,
And gather honey all the day
From every opening flower!

The English language, too, has numerous allusions to bees; 'busy as a bee'; having a 'bee in your bonnet'; 'a hive of industry'. . . and there are plenty more. Why? What is the reason for this long-standing fascination with the bee?

One of the most likely reasons is that, until relatively recently, the workings of a hive and the social order of the bees inside were a source of wonder and puzzlement. How do bees mate? If queens are female and drones are male bees, what sex are worker bees? What goes on inside the hive? Before I answer these questions, I should like to take you briefly through the history of beekeeping; it is a fascinating subject.

The first real record of man's exploitation of honey bees is to be found in Spanish prehistoric cave etchings, dating from approximately 7000 BC. In one of these (see Figs 1 & 1a) a man can be seen climbing up a rope to a cleft in a sheer rock face, to 'rob' the colony of its combs and carry them back down to a friend waiting at the bottom.

Moving on through history we find the first recorded instance of nomadic beekeeping: Ancient Egyptian beekeepers took their

Fig 1   Spanish cave painting

swarms with them when whole populations were moved lock, stock and barrel up or down the River Nile, depending on the season. (This practice can still be seen in parts of modern-day China, although the use of trains as transport makes the whole process much easier!)

It is interesting to note that the Egyptians were as unsure as generations of men were after them as to how bees were pro-created. They believed that bees came from the sun god Ra. Other cultures had equally odd beliefs. Africans believed that they rose out of the bodies of dead lions, while in European folklore the bee is closely linked with death and bees have to be told about a death in the family, otherwise, it is said, they will not produce honey. Given the fact that the bee was first domesticated at the end of the Neolithic period, the evolution of such beliefs is understandable. Whenever man forms close links with a species, superstitions and bizarre ideas flourish about phenomena he does not understand.

Fig 1a   Spanish cave painting detail

Although bees were originally domesticated for their honey, there is ample evidence that they were once used as weapons in several countries: 13th-century Hungary, 17th-century Germany and East Africa as late as the First World War provide examples of such original warfare. It is easy to imagine the havoc which could be wrought by hives of angry bees thrown into the middle of advancing enemy troops!

As far as beekeeping in the United Kingdom is concerned, we know that the Ancient Britons had domesticated colonies in the forests. Indeed, the British Isles were known by the Romans as the 'Honey Isles'.

It was not until the late Middle Ages that the 'skep' was developed. A skep consists of a basket made by stitching together coils of straw rope, and hives of this design are still used in parts of Europe today (see Fig 2). The Tudor House garden in Southampton for example, is a living museum of beekeeping. There the visitor can see not only straw skeps, but also bee bowls which are kept in recesses in a brick wall to protect the hives. The skep, however, was the most commonly used hive and it became quite sophisticated. Although this system bore a close similarity to the way bees live in the wild, with the entrance to the hive at the bottom and the honeycombs at the top, it did not allow for examination of the bee colony.

The modern hive used in most parts of the world is almost identical to one invented by the American clergyman L.L. Langs-

Fig 2 A skep (traditional straw)

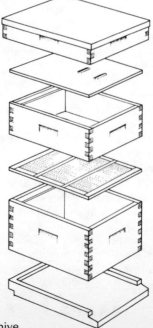

Fig 3 'Langstroth' hive

troth in 1851 (see Fig 3). This hive consists of a set of superimposed boxes inside which bees are kept on hanging comb frames. Between these frames and the box sides is a gap of between 5mm and 9mm, called the 'bee space'. Langstroth discovered that the bees would leave a 5mm gap between the box and the frame and would build the combs up to leave the same gap between them so that the bees could move around the hive. This new system made it possible to lift combs out individually on their frames so that the frames could be moved to different hives if so desired, or so that the condition of the colony could be examined.

Until the 16th century, very little was known about bees — and much of what was thought to be fact at that time turned out to be fallacy. In 1586 the world was shocked to discover that the 'sultan' or 'king' bee was in fact a queen. In the 17th century, it was first suggested that the worker bees were female and the drones male (which in essence is true, although workers only have tiny ovaries and cannot normally produce eggs). However, it was as late as 1845 that a man called Johann Dzierzon realized that drones are produced from unfertilized eggs, whereas workers and queens are produced from fertilized ones. This discovery was the key not only to good hive management but also to understanding the lives of bees.

A honeyed existence

There are three kinds of bee in a honey-bee colony: workers, drones and the queen (see Fig 4). The workers have many duties during their short life, including acting as 'nurses' to the bee larvae in their cells — feeding them and sealing them inside with wax when it is time for them to pupate — ventilating the hive, standing guard at the hive entrances to see off potential intruders and, of course, foraging for pollen and nectar to make honey. This last duty occupies the major part of their short lifespan.

As Dzierzon suggested, the drones are indeed produced from unfertilized eggs laid by the queen. Their sole task is to mate with the queen and, once they have fulfilled that function, the drones are not allowed to return to the hive but are left to die in the inhospitable outside world.

The queen is unique for many reasons, but she is unique in nature in that she can choose the sex of her offspring at will. When she mates with a drone during her mating flight, enough sperm to last her through her egglaying life is deposited in a special sac. She usually begins to lay two eggs within two or three days of returning to the hive from the mating flight. These eggs are not laid at random. When the queen finds a suitable, smallish cell for a worker bee, she inserts her abdomen into the cell and lays an egg which will have been fertilized by the excretion of a very small quantity of sperm.

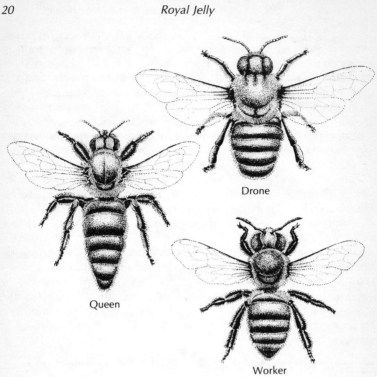

Fig 4 Three bee types: queen, drone and worker

How she prevents the glandular excretion of sperm when laying a 'drone egg' is a mystery, as is much, still, about the queen bee.

So the worker bees develop from fertilized eggs laid in small cells, while the drones evolve from unfertilized eggs laid in larger cells. How, then, are queens produced? The egg which will develop into a queen bee is totally indistinguishable from a 'worker egg' at the time it is laid. The only difference is in the size and shape of the cell. A queen cell is very much larger, stands out from the comb and hangs down from it.

Despite the identical nature of the eggs, there are enormous differences between the queen and the worker by the time they reach maturity. The queen is considerably larger than the worker, has very different inherited instincts and a remarkably different anatomy. Her abdomen is distinctly pointed for egg-laying, she lacks the food glands and the pollen-gathering equipment which worker bees have, she has a larger thorax, is much longer overall, has large, pear-shaped ovaries and a special gland from which she excretes 'queen substance'. This substance contains a combination of fatty acids which are related to the fatty acids found in royal jelly. In the case of the queen, however, the glandular secretions act as a pheromone — a message to all the bees in the colony that the queen is present and all is well. The queen will live for up to six years and lay more than 2,000 eggs per day.

Compare this with the much smaller worker bee whose only reproductive organs are rudimentary ovaries, who has a life expectancy of as little as six weeks and who secretes the magical substance which is the subject of this book — royal jelly.

How, then, is it possible for two eggs which are similar in all respects to develop into two such different insects as the queen and the worker bee? The answer is at once simple and extraordinary — royal jelly.

Until the eggs have hatched into larvae, which takes about three days, nothing remarkable occurs; indeed nothing remarkable occurs for several days afterwards, either. As soon as an egg hatches, be it in a worker or a queen cell, one of the worker bees will secrete a drop of royal jelly from its brood food glands into the cell. Royal jelly is continually deposited in the cell for some two to three days (it has been estimated that a larva is fed up to 1,300 times a day and that feeding during the larval stage may involve more than 2,750 bees).

It is at this point that the difference in the feeding pattern for queens and workers becomes apparent. After three days, worker bee larvae are fed a mixture of royal jelly, honey and pollen, while the future queen still receives her rich diet of royal jelly with nothing added. After eight days, both types of cells are sealed with wax while the larvae spin their cocoons, moult, and change from larvae into pupae. Within the pupae, the adult bees are forming. The worker emerges 21 days after its egg was laid, while the new queen has chewed her way out of her queen cell five days earlier — just 16 days after the egg was laid.

If the new queen meets any other freshly hatched queens, a fight to the death ensues. Otherwise, the virgin queen will scour the hive for any potential rivals still in the pupal stage and will kill them by stinging them through the cell walls. About a week after emerging from her cell (see colour plate section), the queen will embark on her mating flight and the cycle begins again.

Throughout her life the queen will be fed royal jelly by her worker subjects. The only time her diet varies is shortly after she emerges from her cell, when she takes a few sips of honey.

The vital factor

It is clear that the most amazing fact in this account of life within the hive is that royal jelly transforms a worker bee larva destined for a

Cinderella existence into a true queen. This has been a source of great controversy and much research for many years.

The results of this research are fascinating. To begin with, it has been proved many times (indeed, it is now accepted practice in queen-rearing) that a worker bee larva can be transferred to a queen cell before it is three days old and will still grow into a queen. The timing, though, is crucial. If the transfer is left any later, the result will be a bee which is neither queen nor worker, but somewhere between the two.

Nowadays, the scientific community is agreed that royal jelly is the vital factor in the development of a queen bee. Attempts have been made to synthesize royal jelly and to produce queens with the synthetic product in vain. Many of the larvae thus fed die at the pupal stage, and those which survive into adulthood are not full queens but queen/worker hybrids.

Superbees

Intensive research has also centred on the various strains of bee in an attempt to select the best bee for a particular purpose, whether it be for more prolific breeding, greater honey production or lack of aggression. This research has also, of course, involved cross-breeding, i.e. using drones from one strain to mate with queens from another.

There are four species of honey bee: *Apis mellifera*, the most common honey bee in the world; *Apis florea*, a tiny bee found in South-East Asia; *Apis dorsata*, also an inhabitant of South-East Asia but a very large bee which builds extremely large combs; and *Apis cerana*, also called *Apis indica*, which hails from the Indian sub-continent. The last three species are not prolific honey producers and, since man's principal purpose in domesticating bees has been to obtain honey, it is hardly surprising that *Apis mellifera* has become the dominant honey bee (see Fig 5).

Through continuous cross-breeding and mutation over the millennia, more than 20 races of bees have evolved, including the infamous Brazilian-African hybrids which acquired the reputation of being 'killer bees' when they escaped into the wild. At the other end of the aggression scale, however, is the Italian bee, *Apis ligustica*, and it is this honey bee which has attracted the most interest in recent times.

Italian bees are smaller than the original *Apis mellifera*, to which species *Apis ligustica* is closely related, but they have proved to be true superbees. Not only are they renowned for their gentleness, but they are also prolific breeders and honey producers. What is more, they have been found to be superior producers of royal jelly in regard to both quantity and quality. This is extremely fortunate

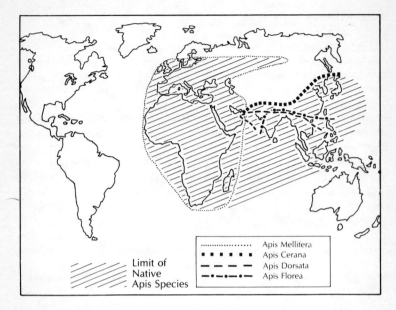

Fig 5   Bee distribution

for the growing number of people around the world who appreciate the benefits of royal jelly as a dietary supplement, since the Italian bee's superiority as a honey producer means that this strain is now established in virtually every country.

As we shall be seeing later, the Chinese in particular adopted the Italian bee for breeding purposes earlier this century, and the majority of the six million domesticated bee colonies in China are now Italian. In this, as in so many other areas of apiculture, China has led the way.

Products of the hives

Of course, royal jelly is not the only bee product used by man. There are many others, of which the best known is honey. For many thousands of years, honey was the only sweetener available to man and it was only as recently as 200 years ago that its modern substitute, sugar, was processed from the sugar cane plant and made widely available. As well as honey, we shall look at three other products of the hive, pollen, propolis and, believe it or not, bee venom.

Honey

Honey is commercially available in three forms — liquid, comb and creamed. The two most frequently found are the liquid and creamed versions.

Bees manufacture honey from the nectar they collect from flowers on their foraging flights. Although, in its natural state, nectar is rather tasteless and contains up to 80 per cent water, once the worker bees have converted it into honey it is rich and sweet, with the water content reduced to about 17 per cent.

As a food, honey is hard to beat. Every part of it can be absorbed by the body and used within one hour. As such it is a source of safe, fast energy and is vastly superior to even raw sugar. Although in an ideal world we would not want our food or drinks sweetened, the truth is that few of us can claim never to crave sweet things so, if you prefer your tea or coffee sweetened, or if you find cooked fruit too tart, try using honey instead of sugar — your body will be grateful!

Apart from its delicious taste, honey also has therapeutic properties in that it soothes raw tissues; this is why a honey and lemon drink is so soothing when you have a sore throat. Honey also helps to retain calcium in the body and this is invaluable for women after the menopause when loss of calcium can lead to osteoporosis. Honey contains a significant amount of potassium, too, which helps to balance acid accumulations in the body, so it can be very useful for sufferers from arthritis and rheumatism.

Pollen

Pollen becomes a talking point every summer when hay fever sufferers keep a close eye on the pollen count to see what kind of day they are going to have; in other words, whether or not they will have to undergo the torture of continuous sneezing, streaming eyes and congestion. On this subject, it is worth noting that royal jelly can prove very helpful in alleviating the suffering of those who are allergic to pollen. A gentleman who had suffered severely with hay fever from the age of 18 began taking fresh royal jelly in October 1986. The following summer saw his symptoms much reduced and he says,

> During the current peak period for hay fever of May, June and July (summer 1988) I have had no symptoms whatsoever, even when spending eight hours walking through fields of grass and wheat at the very peak of the pollen count. This is in contrast to the fact that contact with straw, even during the winter months, for a period in excess of one or two hours would normally have been sufficient to trigger the symptoms before taking royal jelly.

It may surprise the unfortunate folk who suffer from hay fever that, in many parts of the world, pollen is used as a medicine. This is more easily understandable when you learn that it is rich in protein and amino acids and forms, with honey, the basic diet of all the bees in the hive (except, of course, for the queen). Indeed, no one has yet succeeded in 'synthesizing' pollen from other food sources with anything like as nutritious a result.

Propolis

This hive product is the least familiar to the man in the street. It is a sticky material collected by bees from buds or tree bark and used as a type of cement inside the hive, for filling in cracks and smoothing over rough surfaces. Propolis is a mixture of wax, resin, balsam, oil and a little pollen, although its precise make up depends, of course, on the plant source.

Despite the variations in the constituents of propolis, many medical uses have been found for this substance both in Asia and in the West. It seems to act both as an antibiotic and a bactericide, and as such is used in helping wounds to heal. Some practitioners have also found it invaluable in treating skin diseases, while a Russian dentist claimed that it was far superior to cocaine as an anaesthetic. For their part, many French people swear by propolis as a means of getting rid of colds and boosting the immune system.

Propolis has probably been the subject of even less research than royal jelly, but it is clear that there are very strong grounds for such work.

Recently, I was invited to visit the Apitherapy Hospital at Lianyungang in China where only bee products are used in the treatment of patients. There I learned that propolis is used to reduce cholesterol levels in the blood and that the Chinese are actively researching medical applications of all these products of the hive. Hopefully such work will also be carried out in the West soon.

Bee venom

As any beekeeper will tell you, being stung by a bee is always a painful experience, no matter how many years one has been an apiarist. However, bee venom does contain beneficial substances, including carbohydrates, lipids, free amino acids, peptides, proteins and enzymes. The peptides, in particular, have an anti-inflammatory effect, and in that same Apitherapy Hospital honey bees are induced to sting the inflamed joints of arthritic patients. At the same time, the bees are made to sting the patients on the relevant acupuncture points.

Honey, pollen, propolis and bee venom are all remarkable substances which make considerable contributions to the health of human beings. In my view, royal jelly is an even more astonishing substance, both in terms of its make-up and its effects, as the following chapters will show.

CHAPTER 2

——A recipe for success——

You might well think that, since nearly every mystery in the universe has been solved, analysing the ingredients of royal jelly would have been child's play by comparison. Unfortunately, the truth is that one insuperable problem remains: although scientists have succeeded in analysing 96 per cent of the contents of royal jelly, 4 per cent resolutely defies even the most sophisticated technology of this electronic age.

Many of royal jelly's beneficial effects can be explained by reference to its various ingredients, but others appear to have no connection with the known constituents or to be more dramatic than one might expect given the quantities involved. Whether these effects are due to that mystery 4 per cent, no one can say, and theories abound concerning the composition of that tantalizing fraction. Does it, as Professor Fang Zhu of the Lianyungang Apitherapy Hospital believes, contain an antibacterial substance which increases the number of white blood cells? Is it some substance found nowhere else in nature? Certainly, as we shall see, one ingredient in royal jelly *is* found nowhere else.

Whatever the make-up of that mysterious 4 per cent, there is yet another puzzling aspect to royal jelly and that is its synergetic effect. Synergy is a very fashionable word which is often misused, but in the case of royal jelly it is very appropriate, for the effect of the *whole* is indeed greater than that of each *part* taken individually. I asked all the professors I met in China why royal jelly is so beneficial and they replied, without exception, that the benefits could not be traced back to specific ingredients but were the result of all the different ingredients acting together. Royal jelly puts the body's systems back into balance and this is most probably due to the similar balance between the different ingredients which are present in just the right quantities to produce the maximum effect. I should stress at this point that the quantities referred to are very small indeed — there is not the slightest danger of taking an excess of any particular ingredient!

When you remember that it is a 100 per cent natural substance, used as a complete food by one of God's creatures, this all-round balance becomes a perfectly logical phenomenon. After all, if you consider that breast milk contains everything which a baby needs for at least the first six months of its life and that royal jelly contains everything which a queen bee needs for the whole of her life, then the extreme richness of this natural substance in ingredients which are essential to health, development and a balanced metabolism is easier to accept.

Does the fact that royal jelly plays such a crucial part in bee nutrition necessarily mean that it can realistically be mentioned in the same breath as breast milk and accorded a key role in our own nutrition? I believe it does and I can bring one startling piece of evidence to support my belief. In 1966, in the Department of Paediatrics at the University of Florence, 42 infants, including premature babies, were fed royal jelly with impressive results. The babies gained weight, their red corpuscle counts increased and the assimilation of protein into the bloodstream was greater than that induced by any other known treatment of malnutrition.

I should like to take the breast milk analogy a little further. If you were to analyse breast milk from 100 mothers you would find that its composition varied signficantly according to the diet of the mother. There might even be detectable quantities of drugs in the milk if the mother were on certain medication. Now, although, in an ideal world, every baby would have milk from its own mother, babies who are fed from 'milk banks' consisting of donated breast milk fare very well. Indeed, until relatively recently, the practice of wet-nursing was a common one in Western society.

Now let us look at royal jelly. Its composition does differ slightly depending on the diet of the worker bees who produce it. It will vary according to the source of nectar and pollen which the bees bring into the hive and may even contain chemical substances (rather like the drugs in certain mothers' breast milk). However, providing the raw materials for the food end product have not been treated with chemical pesticides or subjected to other environmental pollution, the quality of the royal jelly produced is first-class. The best fresh royal jelly on the market originates in China, where the producers are careful to ensure that the source plants are not polluted by chemicals, but I cannot vouch for the cut-price royal jelly products which have been flooding the market recently.

It may seem a cause for concern that, according to the location of the hive from which the 'bee milk' (as royal jelly is sometimes called) is collected, the composition of the substance will vary. As I have already implied, any chemical plant treatments may contaminate the royal jelly, but also the type of plants from which nectar and pollen are scavenged can subtly alter the end product. In addition to these factors, the precise nature of royal jelly produced by a given worker bee may vary during the insect's feeding life and depends too on the time of year.

However, we have no need to worry. As long as there are no chemical contaminants and the royal jelly is preserved in its fresh state, the effects on our health will be identical, no matter what the plant source of the royal jelly we buy in the shops.

That being said, it is slightly bewildering, but understandable, to see variations in the analyses of royal jelly which have been issued by the world's laboratories. It is therefore worth looking at all these analyses when deciding which are the proven constituents of royal jelly. Certain elements are always present, whereas others may occur only rarely, according to the prevailing climatic conditions and the geographical location of the bee colony from which the substance was collected.

A good basis for discussion is the representative analysis produced in 1986 by the Cardiff County Public Health Laboratory, given below.

Water	24.00%	(weight in weight)
Carbohydrates	15.00%	(w/w)
Nitrogen	50.00%	(w/w)
(equivalent to	31.00%	(w/w) of protein)
Phosphorus	0.70%	(w/w)
Sulphur	0.40%	(w/w)
Mineral matter	2.00%	(w/w)

The mineral matter contains the following trace elements: iron, manganese, nickel, cobalt, silicon, chromium, gold, mercury, bismuth and arsenic.

The following vitamins are present:

Vitamin B1 (thiamine)	1.2 –7.40 mg/100 gm
Vitamin B2 (riboflavin)	5.2 –10.00 mg/100 gm
Vitamin B3 (niacin)	60.0 –150.00 mg/100 gm
Vitamin B5 (pantothenic acid)	65.0 –200.00 mg/100 gm
Vitamin B6 (pyridoxine)	2.2 –10.20 mg/100 gm
Vitamin B12 (cyanocobalamin)	0.15 mg/100 gm
Vitamin C (ascorbic acid)	12.0 mg/100 gm
Vitamin H (biotin)	0.9 –3.70 mg/100 gm
Inositol	80.0 –150.00 mg/100 gm
Folic acid	0.2 mg/100 gm

Before I go any further, I think that I ought to deal with two items in the above analysis which may have readers throwing their hands up in horror and their valuable royal jelly into the dustbin. Yes, royal jelly may contain traces of mercury and arsenic, but there is not the slightest need to panic. To begin with, both are present in such tiny quantities as to be hardly worth mentioning, but I would also wager that most people are unaware that we all have both mercury and arsenic in our bodies already.

Arsenic, in particular, has gained a very bad press due to its one-time popularity as a way of disposing of one's nearest but not dearest and also undesirable rodents. Although arsenic is a very powerful poison, it is only toxic when administered in the pure chemical state. When it is combined with other substances it loses its toxicity and any surplus arsenic not needed by our bodies is simply excreted. You may think that we do not actually *need* to have arsenic in our bodies, but even scientists are not sure of this — witness the fact that it has been classified as a mineral which is 'possibly essential', meaning that a *lack* of arsenic may perhaps be harmful! It is also worth noting that for many years arsenic was a common pharmaceutical ingredient and is still used in homoeopathy. Whether these metals are essential or not, our bodies need to be cleansed of any excess. This job is done very efficiently by vitamin C, which royal jelly contains, of course!

I should now like to look at what all the various 'ingredients' detected by the Cardiff laboratory can do for us. You may find this long list daunting, but I do not intend that you should read it right through at one sitting; rather, you should dip into it, using it as a reference source. Indeed, if you were to study the attributes of each ingredient in royal jelly, you would probably become convinced that you were suffering from a deficiency of every one. It's rather like studying a medical dictionary — all the symptoms seem worryingly familiar!

Carbohydrates

There was a time when the word 'carbohydrates' struck fear into the heart of weight-watchers everywhere, but today the chief enemy of slimmers has been identified as saturated fat. Indeed, carbohydrates have vital work to do in the body: they are energy-producing compounds which keep our blood sugar levels up and help the body to store protein. The carbohydrates in royal jelly are composed mainly of sugars.

Nitrogen

People rarely talk about nitrogen when discussing nutrition, but without it we would not have proteins, and we all know about the importance of proteins: they are necessary for life. Strictly speaking however, it is not the proteins which are vital to us, but rather the amino acids, which are the building blocks of protein. The other 'ingredient' in proteins is, in fact, nitrogen: the nitrogen bonds with the various amino acids to form proteins. As you can see from the Cardiff analysis, the proportion of protein in royal jelly is considerable, so the amino acids which it contains are well worth analysing and discussing.

Amino acids

The protein content of royal jelly has been analysed by many laboratories and most of the amino acids known to man have been detected, including alanine, arginine, aspartic acid, glutamic acid, glycine, histidine, isoleucine, leucine, lysine, phenylalanine, proline, serine, threonine, tyrosine and valine.

Amino acids are classified as 'essential' or 'non-essential', not according to whether we need them for our health (we need them all), but according to whether our bodies can manufacture them or not. The 'essential' amino acids are the ones which we cannot synthesize ourselves and which therefore have to be obtained from our food intake or from dietary supplements.

As with many other supplements, there would be no point in taking amino acids on their own, since our bodies need vitamins B6, B12 and niacin to be present before the amino acids can be used. If you glance at the analysis of royal jelly given above, you will see that all three are present. This underlines the importance of not looking at the ingredients of royal jelly in isolation — it is the combination of them all which makes royal jelly such a perfectly-balanced, nutritious and highly effective substance.

So, let us look at what some of these amino acids can do for us when, as in royal jelly, they are present with the various other ingredients needed for them to play their full part in keeping us healthy.

Arginine

Arginine is particularly important to men as it helps to increase their sperm count and therefore can help with sub-fertility problems. It is also vital for every adult whether male or female from the age of 30 onwards, since the pituitary gland stops secreting this substance at that time. You may think that this does not matter, but arginine is needed to synthesize and release growth hormone from the pituitary gland, and it is this hormone which helps to keep our weight stable and our figures in shape!

Aspartic acid

Royal jelly contains a relatively large proportion of this amino acid which has two functions. Firstly, it eliminates excess ammonia from the body, thereby protecting the central nervous system. Secondly (and probably more importantly since the end result is so noticeable), it is an energy booster. Research carried out in the l970s revealed that when athletes are given aspartic acid salts their stamina is noticeably increased. It would appear that aspartic acid is partly responsible for the energizing effect of royal jelly.

Glutamic acid

Glutamic acid has a somewhat similar function to aspartic acid. It too affects ammonia but, rather than eliminate it from the body, it converts ammonia into glutamine. Now this is another 'wonder substance', in that it is believed that it is able to raise IQs. This would seem enough of an achievement for a single amino acid, but it can also help with alcoholism, speed up healing, and it has a beneficial effect on depression, fatigue and sexual impotence. Glutamic acid and glycine (see below) are also believed to perform a vital role when combined in delaying ageing, building up the body's resistance to tumours, relieving allergies and helping with diabetes, hypoglycaemia and arthritis, as well as alleviating the side-effects of chemotherapy and radiation in the treatment of cancer.

Glycine

A sweet-tasting amino acid, glycine also has several strings to its bow. It boosts the pituitary gland function and muscle function, which accounts for its use in the treatment of muscular dystrophy. It is also used to treat patients with hypoglycaemia (low blood sugar) and is included in many antacid medicines.

Histidine

Although this amino acid is synthesized in the body, it is categorized as an essential one for infants and children since it cannot be manufactured in adequate quantities during periods of rapid growth.

Lysine

Lysine is one of the essential amino acids and it is especially helpful for those people who find it hard to concentrate, are losing their hair, or suffer dizzy spells, as they may be suffering from a lysine deficiency. Lysine's main functions are tissue repair, aiding growth, and producing hormones, enzymes and antibodies.

Phenylalanine

This is another of the essential amino acids and it plays a vital role in our bodies. It is a neuro-transmitter, sending signals from our nerve cells to our brains. When you increase your phenylalanine consumption, you should find any depression lifting, your memory and general mental capacity improving, your appetite for food decreasing and your appetite for sex increasing! That's quite a repertoire for one little amino acid, but this is one of those essential acids which we cannot manufacture for ourselves, so it is evidently very important that we have our daily dose, if not from our diet then by means of a royal jelly capsule.

Tyrosine

Tyrosine is not an essential amino acid, but it is closely linked with phenylalanine and, like all the amino acids, is vital to our health. Some phenylalanine is transformed into tyrosine in our bodies to perform the mood-lifting and appetite-suppressing functions. If the phenylalanine is needed elsewhere, not enough tyrosine will be provided to do these jobs, and we would be suffering from a tyrosine deficiency, with consequent depression and increased appetite: not an attractive prospect!

——————————— Minerals ———————————

To show the importance of minerals in our body, it is interesting to look at the major elements which make up the human body and how they combine:

Oxygen 65 per cent
Carbon 18 per cent
Hydrogen 10 per cent
Minerals 3.5 per cent
Nitrogen 3 per cent

About 90 per cent of the oxygen combines with 7 per cent of the hydrogen to make water, which accounts for an astonishing two-thirds of our body weight. Then the two minerals sulphur and phosphorus act with the rest of the hydrogen and oxygen, as well as some of the carbon and nitrogen, to make our 'organic compounds' — fats, proteins, carbohydrates, etc — which alone constitute 90 per cent of the solid parts of our body.

We constantly hear about the importance of vitamins for health, but minerals are even more important, for two reasons. To begin with, we can manufacture vitamins in our bodies, but we cannot manufacture minerals. If the minerals are not in our food, then we go without. With the advent of refined foods and the use of commercial fertilizers, the amount of minerals in our food and in much of the soil used for food production is out of balance. Even a slight alteration in the level of important minerals can have a drastic effect on our health.

So, let us look at the various minerals in royal jelly, beginning with the two main ones — phosphorus and sulphur.

Phosphorus

The bulk of the phosphorus in our bodies is in our bones, but this mighty mineral plays a very important role in other areas, too. One of its most interesting functions, given the beneficial effect of royal jelly in this respect, is in keeping the skin, hair and nails in peak condition. Improvement in all three is often one of the first benefits observed by those who take fresh royal jelly regularly. Also, phosphorus is required by the nervous system, to protect it from stress and to improve brain function. This is the reason for fish being called 'brain food' since it is particularly rich in phosphorus. Phosphorus tones up our circulation and is needed to process carbohydrates and fats.

In many of these tasks, phosphorus combines with calcium and, although the Cardiff analysis of royal jelly's constituents does not include it, many other royal jelly analyses *have* indeed identified large amounts of calcium. This discrepancy is probably due to the differences in honey-bee diets, as I mentioned earlier in this chapter.

Sulphur

Think of sulphur and you probably think of matches; indeed, it may be somewhat alarming to ponder on the fact that our bodies contain a mineral which is used in making fire! However, sulphur, like so many minerals, is invaluable to us and has a host of beneficial properties. It speeds up our metabolisms, cleans out our digestive tracts, oxidizes our blood and has a dynamic effect on many skin conditions, including psoriasis and acne. This last will ring a bell with many users of royal jelly and Vitamin E cream, since many skin conditions respond magnificently to the cream as well as to royal jelly taken internally.

Another interesting fact about sulphur is that the hormone insulin is a sulphur compound. In an American study, Kramer et al isolated peptides from royal jelly which had very similar properties to human insulin. Whether these peptides act like insulin in humans has yet to be established and could be a fruitful area for further research.

Trace minerals

The 'trace minerals' are, as the term suggests, present in only small quantities in our bodies. Do not be misled into thinking that they are unimportant, and that it does not matter if we do not get enough of them. They *are* important, and it *does* matter. If you are baking a sponge using plain flour with baking powder as a raising agent, and you leave the baking powder out, the result will be a very flat cake. The baking powder may be only a tiny part of the ingredients as far as relative quantities are concerned, but without it, the recipe will be a failure. The same applies to trace minerals: we may need only a tiny amount of them, but without that tiny amount our bodies will not function properly.

Iron Most people are aware that our bodies need iron, and that a lack of it causes anaemia. With iron-deficiency anaemia, there is not enough oxygen-carrying haemoglobin. This means that the red blood cells become pale and smaller so that they cannot distribute oxygen efficiently around the body. The result is physical tiredness, depression, forgetfulness and reduced mental functions.

The iron in royal jelly seems to do its job well, since royal jelly has been shown in several experiments to boost haemoglobin levels considerably. There is, however, another ingredient in royal jelly which plays a key part in raising haemoglobin levels, (see page 40).

Manganese Nobody has as yet identified the effects of a deficiency of manganese in humans, although poultry lacking this mineral do not grow to their full size and have bone abnormalities, reproductive problems and anaemia. It is thought that one effect of manganese deficiency may be an increased tendency towards diabetes.

Nickel Nickel is not, as far as we know, essential to our well-being. That being said, it is found in newborn babies and, since nature always seems to know best, it may well be that nickel plays a part in tissue building.

Cobalt Cobalt is naturally present in vitamin B12, contained in royal jelly. Whether all the cobalt is present in this form has not been ascertained. Cobalt is used in hospitals to treat deep-seated cancers and it may be that the cobalt in B12 acts in a similar fashion, hunting out and destroying precancerous or cancerous cells, although this is open to question. Certainly it would be logical to assume that cobalt may have that function when present in vitamin B12, and that in so acting it might offer some protection against cancer.

Silicon The value of this mineral has only recently been appreciated It is instrumental in preventing the progress of arthritic diseases and, like phosphorus, it contributes to healthy nails and hair. This clever trace mineral also keeps the protective sheaths round our nerve fibres in tip-top condition.

Chromium Chromium, like manganese, seems to have a link with diabetes. Without it, insulin cannot do its job and our bodies cannot metabolize cholesterol. The effect of chromium deficiency can be seen when we compare the results of a traditional Japanese diet with those of a modern Western one. The Japanese have five times as much chromium in their bodies as we do, and consequently suffer less from diabetes and hardened arteries. Sadly, with the introduction of our 'fast food' culture, the incidence of such life-threatening conditions is now increasing.

Gold and bismuth Neither of these minerals plays any part in human nutrition, or at least, no use has yet been identified for them! However, in small amounts they are not toxic, either. Bismuth is, in fact, used in some proprietary stomach medicines, while gold injections are occasionally used to treat arthritis.

Before I leave the topic of minerals, it is worth mentioning that nearly all the essential minerals and trace elements have been detected in royal jelly at one time or another, including calcium, potassium, copper, zinc, sodium and magnesium.

Vitamins

I am sure vitamins need hardly any introduction. Multi-vitamin supplements crowd the shelves of chemists and healthfood shops, and are becoming increasingly common sights in supermarkets. We all know about vitamin C's role in combating colds, and it is more or less common knowledge that vitamin B6 is very helpful in treating pre-menstrual tension.

Here again, we should remember that it is pointless to take many artificially-produced dietary supplements in isolation. Vitamins, like minerals, interact with other vitamins or minerals to produce a required effect, and a lack of any given vitamin may also involve a lack of others.

Come to that, it has been shown that synthetic supplements can throw the body's balance completely out of kilter, whereas natural sources of vitamins and minerals somehow do not have this deleterious effect. What we are all striving for is a perfect balance, and only by taking a well-balanced, wholly natural supplement can we hope to achieve this result. Royal jelly may not be the only natural substance to offer a recipe for success, but, rather like oil of evening primrose, it not only seems to be good for us, but also has dramatic effects on a range of ailments — without side effects! What more could one ask for?

Vitamin B1 (thiamine)

We need thiamine to convert carbohydrates into mental and physical energy. Children, in particular, need plenty of this vitamin as they are growing. If you are lacking in thiamine, you may well feel tired and depressed, have difficulty concentrating, and have little interest in food. Symptoms of a severe deficiency are swollen ankles and pins and needles in your lower limbs, though, of course both of these may be attributable to other causes.

Vitamin B2 (riboflavin)

Once upon a time, our diet was rich in vitamin B2 from unpasteurized milk, free-range eggs and other dairy produce which had not been 'tampered' with. Because of modern production methods, our riboflavin intake has been reduced dramatically, resulting in cracked lips, mouth ulcers, sore eyes and dermatitis. As with a lack of thiamine, a vitamin B2 deficiency can also result in depression and apathy. Clearly, we are doing ourselves an enormous favour if we make sure that we have enough of both these vital vitamins.

Vitamin B3 (niacin)

If you thought that the symptoms of thiamine and riboflavin deficiency were bad enough, wait until you have read what those poor people who go short of niacin could suffer (and I am talking about roughly half the population!). Indigestion, stomach pains, irritability, forgetfulness, headaches, swollen gums, insomnia, swollen tongue, loss of appetite, dermatitis, dizziness, tiredness, nausea and nervousness are some of the symptoms: it's not a very pretty picture, is it? Severe deficiency, which is admittedly rare these days produces pellagra, a particularly unpleasant disease characterized by diarrhoea, dementia and chronic dermatitis. Also if you are a smoker, you should know that the nicotine in your cigarettes releases adrenalin into your body and, if your niacin levels are low, your adrenal gland becomes very confused and starts sending equally confused messages round your nervous system!

Vitamin B5 (pantothenic acid)

Pantothenic acid is a relatively recent subject for research, and it has been found to have many startling properties. One of the most startling is that prematurely greying hair can be restored to its normal colour if the cause of the greying was a vitamin B5 deficiency! This may surprise you, but I can well believe this discovery since I have heard of several cases of grey hair reverting to its original colour after a course of royal jelly capsules.

I have been describing what is, of course, purely a cosmetic benefit, but it does reflect the fact that royal jelly is the richest natural source of vitamin B5. White, Handler and Smith in *Principles of Biochemistry* say,

In general the distribution of pantothenic acid resembles that of the other B vitamins; yeast, liver and eggs are among the richest sources . . . royal jelly (prepared by the bee colony for the nutrition of the queen bee), and fish ovaries (before spawning) are the richest known sources of this vitamin.

What else can pantothenic acid do for us, apart from contributing to attractive locks? Its most important use is in treating arthritis, and I shall be looking at this in detail in Chapter Seven. In addition to this, vitamin B5 helps wounds to heal, fights infection, prevents fatigue and alleviates dermatitis. If you have insufficient pantothenic acid in your diet, you may well have symptoms of hypoglycaemia, blood or skin disorders, and even duodenal ulcers.

Vitamin B6 (pyridoxine)

Vitamin B6 is another very versatile aid to health. It is indispensable in the production of red blood cells and antibodies and can relieve the misery of morning sickness in pregnant women. Also, pyridoxine keeps the nervous system and the skin in peak condition, as well as helping with the digestion of fats and proteins. As I mentioned in the introduction to this section, vitamin B6 has proved helpful in the treatment of pre-menstrual tension. Anaemia and dematitis can result from a deficiency of this vitamin, so you owe it to yourself to make sure you get your daily quota!

Vitamin B12 (cyanocobalamin)

You may be thinking by now that anaemia can be a symptom of almost any vitamin deficiency, and the facts on vitamin B12 will only serve to reinforce this notion. Yes, anaemia can be caused by B12 deficiency too, in addition to general tiredness, irritability and poor brain function.

This vitamin has been used to treat a wide variety of disorders, from coeliac disease to muscular dystrophy, but it is more generally given to increase energy levels, improve the condition of the blood and the nervous system, and to stimulate growth and appetite in children.

Vitamin C (ascorbic acid)

I have some more bad news for smokers: every cigarette you smoke depletes your vitamin C reserves considerably. If you smoke 20 a day, you will need to eat 40 oranges during the day to keep your vitamin C intake up at the level required for health! Alcohol has a similarly destructive effect on vitamin C: even if you drink only occasionally, you will need to boost your intake of this valuable vitamin.

Vitamin C has a reputation for being the arch enemy of the cold virus, although this claim has still not been satisfactorily proven. What is indisputable is that vitamin C is vital for the growth and repair of body tissues: in fact, it works best as a tissue repairer and wound healer when taken with vitamin B12.

If you are not getting enough of this precious vitamin, your gums are probably spongy and bleed easily, your teeth in poor condition and your face a mass of tiny broken veins.

Vitamin H (biotin)

The symptoms of biotin deficiency will sound familiar by now: restricted growth, dermatitis and anaemia. This vitamin is destroyed by egg whites, antibiotics and alcohol, so if you have any of these three regularly, you should increase your biotin intake with royal jelly.

But is biotin that important? Yes, it is. Due to its sulphur content, biotin boosts our resistance to infections, as sulphur is the main cleansing agent in our bodies. Also, biotin is needed if fats and proteins are to be metabolized efficiently, and it helps to keep our skin clear and healthy. It is believed that vitamin H may even aid in preventing premature baldness.

Inositol

One of inositol's most important functions is to combine with choline to form lecithin which metabolizes fats and cholesterol, thus warding off coronary disease. Lecithin also has an uncanny ability to redistribute fat around the body which can be useful if you have too much fat in all the wrong places! Inositol will also make sure that your hair is healthy and glossy while at the same time helping anyone who is prone to eczema.

If you drink a lot of coffee or tea, the inositol in your body will be struggling to do its job, so you will be particularly susceptible to eczema and problems of fat intolerance.

Folic acid

Folic acid is sometimes referred to as vitamin M and must be in correct balance in a woman's body if she is to conceive and in ample supply during the months that follow. Elderly people are also known to require more folic acid than the rest of the population.

This is one of the many vitamins which are destroyed by heat and storage so, if you rarely eat freshly picked raw green vegetables, mushrooms and beans, you are probably short of folic acid. Also, if you drink more than moderate quantities of alcohol you will be destroying any folic acid in your system and could develop a severe vitamin M deficiency, running the risk of developing nutritional megaloblastic anaemia as well as digestive disorders.

Hormones

I mentioned earlier the presence of insulin-like peptides in royal jelly. An equally startling discovery has been made by scientists in recent years: some samples of royal jelly have been found to contain the male sex hormone testosterone. This would obviously be good news for men, but you will be relieved to learn that it would also be good news for women. We all, men and women, contain both female and male hormones, but in different proportions of course. In women, testosterone is produced in small quantities in the ovaries and adrenal cortex to stimulate the female libido. No, women who take royal jelly will not develop beards and hairs on their chests, but they may have an even more enjoyable love life!

The magical fatty acid

You would be forgiven for thinking by now that royal jelly almost has too many marvellous ingredients for its own good, and it *is* difficult to believe that any natural substance can have quite so many beneficial properties (and yet still be scorned by many in the scientific community). However, there is yet another miracle worker hidden away inside royal jelly, and this is a fatty acid with the imposing name of hydroxydecanoic acid.

One remarkable fact about this fatty acid is that it appears nowhere else in nature. Another is that it shows clear bactericidal properties. In tests carried out as long ago as the 1930s, hydroxydecanoic acid was found to kill the harmful organisms *Escherichia coli* and *Salmonella typhosa*. These findings were confirmed 30 years later when Blum and his colleagues discovered that penicillin was only four times as powerful on some organisms as this fatty acid, and that the acid had approximately the same power relationship with chlorotetracycline.

Another benefit of hydroxydecanoic acid proved to be a yeast-inhibiting function, which could be helpful for sufferers of such annoying and sometimes debilitating conditions as thrush and athlete's foot.

At the end of the 1950s, came an even more astonishing finding. Townsend and his co-workers demonstrated that both fresh royal jelly and pure hydroxydecanoic acid prevented the development of transplantable leukaemia, and that they could even prevent the development of abdominal tumours in mice. Part of the reason for this leukaemia inhibition may lie in the fact that royal jelly improves both the number and condition of white blood cells. In fact, hydroxydecanoic acid seems to have an all-round beneficial effect on the blood, as it has been found to increase the haemoglobin content in the red blood cells as well.

I am sure you will agree after this exhaustive analysis of the common ingredients of royal jelly that if a nutritionist were to sit down and try to devise a perfect all-round dietary supplement, he would come up with one which was not that far removed from royal jelly! However, no one has yet succeeded in producing a synthetic supplement which even comes close to the 'perfect' solution. How fortunate we are, therefore, that Mother Nature has seen fit to provide us with a ready-made recipe for success, complete with all the benefits which are unique to natural foods, such as a lack of side-effects, perfect compatibility and interaction between the many ingredients!

CHAPTER 3

—— A consumer's guide ——

Now that I have described all the good things in royal jelly and what they can do for you, you are probably wondering where you can obtain it and in which form you should take it.

As for where royal jelly is on sale, you will find the basic products, described below, in most leading chemists, health food shops and department stores. With regard to the form in which you should take your royal jelly, the first consideration, which I cannot over-emphasize, is that you should take it *fresh*, not freeze-dried. I shall be explaining the scientific basis for this recommendation in Chapter 5, but to my mind and the mind of thousands of other people there really is no comparison between the two as far as potency and effectiveness are concerned.

You could be tempted to use freeze-dried royal jelly because it is substantially cheaper, but in the realm of royal jelly you really do get what you pay for. This maxim applies even to products containing fresh royal jelly, because purity, quality and the *amount* of fresh royal jelly in the product will all affect the retail price. Another factor which is reflected in the product's price is the type of preservative used. I have always been convinced that only natural preservatives can keep fresh royal jelly in peak condition, and my conviction is still as firm as ever. Some of the less expensive brands in the shops use cheap, unsuitable preservatives which enable the price to be kept down, but at the expense of quality!

If you have never used royal jelly before, my advice is to begin with the essential ingredient of any royal jelly regime — the daily capsule.

———————— Royal jelly capsules ————————

To gain long-term benefits from royal jelly, you have to take it long term, too. This is why nearly everyone I know who swears by royal jelly uses the capsules as a basic essential of daily life, taking one capsule first thing in the morning on an empty stomach.

You will not see the effects instantly; in fact, I recommend that you take a 3-month course of capsules before you decide whether royal jelly is for you or not. Some people feel the difference after only a week or two, whereas others have to wait that much longer before they notice a change for the better. There are two reasons for this disparity. Firstly, individuals' metabolisms differ, both in the speed of reaction and in the degree to which they are out of balance and, secondly, some people are more sensitive to changes in their bodies.

Usually, the first improvement noticed is in energy levels. A Corby lady began taking the capsules with very low expectations.

I didn't honestly believe royal jelly would do anything for me. But I seem to have a burst of energy and get up and go, and well, it's lasting. I am cleaning the house from top to bottom, and am eager to get on with the garden. I am even having to curb my enthusiasm to get on with one job after another. I wouldn't have believed it!

More intransigent problems may take longer to respond, but it is worth being patient since there seems to be virtually no limit to the conditions which royal jelly can improve. I have been amazed to hear of several ladies (including a no-nonsense business executive) who are convinced that their grey hair is reverting to its original colour because they have taken royal jelly capsules!

Despite the fact that the capsules are meant to be taken internally, some ingenious people have used them in other ways to good effect. A Cumbrian enthusiast split open a capsule and applied the contents to a troublesome cold sore. He said 'I was amazed how quickly my cold sore cleared up! (A noticeable improvement in about five hours in fact!)'

What is in them?

You will find that most capsules contain 100 – 500 mg of royal jelly: the optimum dosage is 150 mg. Usually, the substance is mixed with other ingredients such as soya bean oil, hydrogenated vegetable oil, beeswax, soya lecithin and other plant extracts. The coating of these capsules is generally made of gelatin.

Remember when you are shopping around for capsules to look for ones which contain *fresh* royal jelly, if possible preserved in honey and wheatgerm oil, since these are the most effective preservatives. Such capsules may seem expensive, but when you think about the price, it is the equivalent per month of a cheap restaurant meal or a seat at the theatre. The cost also compares favourably with that of a visit to the hairdresser, or a jar of top-quality face cream. By the time you have been taking the capsules for a few months, your hair and skin will be in such good condition that you will probably be saving money in that department anyway.

Part of the reason for the relatively high cost of fresh royal jelly capsules is that, in addition to the fact that fresh royal jelly is dear, the technology required to preserve and encapsulate this very volatile substance in its fresh state is itself expensive. However, almost all those who have tried both the freeze-dried and the fresh versions are more than happy to pay the extra money for those extra benefits which they derive from fresh royal jelly.

How can you tell whether the capsules are working?

It is often the case that, when people start taking royal jelly capsules, an improvement in their general health occurs so gradually that they begin to wonder whether it is worth carrying on taking them. One lady from Edinburgh came to just that conclusion.

> I took the capsules for 3 months and noticed no amazing transformation in myself. I was then away on holiday and had taken no supply with me. When I returned I had lost the habit of the daily dose, and in the following weeks I lost the glow and zest which had crept up on me so subtly that I hadn't realized the benefits which that tiny capsule had given me.
>
> My skin and hair protested, and my nails split and flaked. I'm glad to say that I'm now re-established on my routine of the 'golden glow'.

A Middlesex sceptic had a similar experience.

> I stopped taking royal jelly thinking it had not worked in any way. It was when my hairdresser commented that my hair and nail growth had dramatically slowed down that I immediately started taking royal jelly again.
>
> From having a negative attitude towards royal jelly, I am now positive that it works. Today my hair and nails, tomorrow who knows!

The moral of these tales is that, even if you cannot notice any improvement, give the capsules time and try to remember how you were before you started taking them. It would be a good idea to keep a diary for a few months so that you can monitor your progress and have a more objective view, with hindsight, of the effectiveness of royal jelly. If you are still unconvinced, stop taking the capsules for a few weeks — I can guarantee that you will notice the difference, as the benefits slowly accrued over the months evaporate within a week or two!

——————— Royal jelly with honey ———————

Royal jelly and honey products are invaluable for three groups of people: vegetarians, who cannot take capsules because of the gelatin casing; the very young, who have not yet learned how to swallow a capsule; and anyone, including the very elderly, who experiences difficulty in swallowing pills or capsules.

As with the capsules, you will find a wide variation in the prices of these products. This is not because some hold freeze-dried royal jelly while others contain the fresh variety since, as honey is one of the easiest ways of preserving royal jelly, most contain the fresh substance. However, there *is* a difference in the proportion of royal jelly, so you would do well to check the labels carefully before buying. Look out for a product which will provide 150 mg of fresh royal jelly per teaspoonful, as this is the optimum daily dosage. If the quantity of royal jelly is not marked, steer clear — it probably means that there is merely a 'token' amount.

In addition to honey, these royal jelly products usually contain bee pollen and vitamin C, a really palatable and vitalizing mixture! The sweetness of royal jelly with honey makes it a delicious breakfast time spread, or it can even be taken from a spoon, so it is a really easy and pleasant way for all the family to take their daily dose of royal jelly. The one thing you should *not* do is add the product to a hot drink as this will destroy the beneficial properties of the royal jelly.

I recently received a letter about a typical royal jelly and honey family from a mum in Rutland.

I have two small children of 5 and 3 years and have started giving them a spoonful every morning and the benefits are most noticeable. The eldest was finding it difficult to cope with school until he started the honey — he now has the energy to last the day and is less prone to throw his hands up and admit defeat so easily. . . he has managed to remain cold-free despite the sneezes and snuffles going round school. With the little girl the benefits are more pronounced — to put it bluntly, she is a little ratbag without her daily spoonful. We ran out of the honey one Friday and the weekend was dreadful with her tantrums and arguments. After a few days back on the honey she was back to her cheerful and less tired outlook.

I also have a spoonful every morning and it certainly helps me. I seem to have more energy to cope with the children and the driving job I have. In fact I take a jar with me and when I find myself flagging I have another spoonful!

—————— Liquid royal jelly tonic ——————

For a really fast-acting 'pick-me-up' there is nothing to beat royal jelly tonic. The tonic consists of fresh royal jelly, mixed with several other energizing ingredients, and it is packaged in single-dose phials. Many people find that the tonic begins to work within minutes, giving an energizing effect which lasts throughout the day, while others find a gradual increase in their energy levels until a stable peak is reached. Whatever the case, the boost given to sluggish systems is dramatic.

Strangely, this injection of energy does not prevent you from sleeping when the time comes, despite the fact that you feel as though you could keep going for ever. A Northampton lady, who was already taking royal jelly capsules daily, put the tonic to the test.

> I had been to two parties on consecutive nights; the first party ended at 4.30 am, the second at 6 am. On the third night I was faced with yet another party which I knew would also last well into the next day. I felt like death — and looked like it, I may add. The thought of going anywhere but bed had me contemplating suicide!! To the amusement of my husband, children and babysitter, I drank the liquid tonic. I went to the party, I danced all night, had a wonderful time and got to bed at 4.30 am. Now, if that wasn't *the* test, I don't know what is!

Even later in life, when we expect to be able to sit back and watch the grass grow, there are still days when we need an energy booster. Mrs B. from Macclesfield writes,

> Last week I had need to do a very strenuous few days of driving — 900 miles in three days. When I arrived back home at 9.15p.m. my friends volunteered how fresh I looked, showing no signs of expected strain at my age of 70 years! Then I told them I had taken just one small teaspoonful of liquid royal jelly tonic for each of the last three mornings. 'No wonder!' they said.

When you look at what these liquid pick-me-ups contain, it is hardly surprising that they have such a dramatic effect. The most effective kind contains 50 per cent fresh royal jelly — approximately 0.5 g, or up to five times as much royal jelly as is contained in some capsules. It is perfectly all right to take this quantity of royal jelly when a special energy boost is required, but I would not recommend anyone to take 0.5 g every day. That is not to say that such a daily dose has been shown to cause any serious side-effects.

However, you may find that you have rather more energy than is desirable! In any event, such a dosage taken on a daily basis is simply not necessary. The royal jelly is blended with honey, which adds to the energizing capacity of the tonic, as well as ginseng, plant extracts of *damiana aphrodisiaca* and saw palmetto, a trace of capsicum and almond essence.

Ginseng is extracted from the roots of the plant *Panax ginseng* (see Fig 6) and is probably most famous for its role in increasing sexual appetites, but it is also effective in fighting depression and fatigue, resulting in a boost in both physical and mental energy. The Chinese, of course, have used ginseng for thousands of years in their medicines, and Russian cosmonauts have used it too to increase their resistance to stress and fatigue.

Incidentally, both ginseng and *damiana aphrodisiaca* are believed to relieve some of the unpleasant symptoms experienced during the menopause, Ginseng, in particular, contains estriol, a form of oestrogen, so there would seem to be a scientific basis for its helpfulness during the menopause, when a lack of oestrogen produces so many unpleasant symptoms.

However, I should point out that the liquid royal jelly tonic is not intended to be taken every day; far from it. Rather it has been formulated as a supplement to the daily capsule, to be used only occasionally, when you are planning to undertake unusually strenuous physical or mental activity.

Fig 6 Ginseng

Skincare

One of the first results noticed by those who take fresh royal jelly is that the condition of their skin, nails and hair improves dramatically. It was therefore a logical step to try applying royal jelly externally to skin rashes and lesions. The outcome was very encouraging so, a few years ago, one of the first skin creams containing this effective salve was produced.

Royal jelly & vitamin E cream

The most successful of these royal jelly creams is blended with vitamin E, as well as jojoba oil and beeswax. When taken internally, vitamin E has a longstanding reputation for protecting cells as they divide and multiply. More recently, its role when used in ointments to help heal ulcers, burns and cuts has been highlighted. As such, this vitamin has similar properties to royal jelly, and the combination of these two active ingredients has produced some remarkable results.

It was initially intended that royal jelly cream be used on the face and neck, but many purchasers tried it on other parts of their body with considerable success, For example, a concert pianist has discovered that the cream can even safeguard his livelihood.

> My finger tips, which were often chapped and cracked, particularly in cold weather, have completely healed and are no longer giving me any trouble. Having to play the piano in recitals and when teaching I have for years suffered much pain and frustration which has now completely disappeared.

As you will discover in Chapter 7, both royal jelly & vitamin E cream and royal jelly capsules can have dramatic effects on severe eczema, psoriasis and other skin conditions. One lady achieved startling results when she used the cream on a cyst. She had consulted her doctor who told her that she would have to have it excised when it became uncomfortable. Although the lump on her wrist was already painful, since my correspondent was about to go on holiday she decided to wait until she returned before seeing a specialist. I shall let her take up the story.

> The lump got bigger and bigger and was making my arm ache as well, so I thought I would try rubbing some of the cream on it morning and evening. This I did for a while and then one morning I woke up and found the lump had gone right down. Then the lump started to come again a week ago so once again I have been putting the cream on and the lump has gone down again!

Fortunately, most of us are free from such worrying complaints, but still we can derive great benefit from the soothing and revitalizing properties of the cream. A happy lady from Surrey says, 'After using royal jelly & vitamin E cream for about three months. . . friends, relatives — even the beauty consultants at various stores — have all commented on my skin, saying how it glows.' Another lady had found that her skin reacted to all the creams she had tried in the past: 'Everything I tried only made my itchy, sensitive skin that much worse. However, after a day out in the frosty cold my skin was so sore and flaky. I tried the cream and found to my surprise how soothing it was — and no itching!'

An even more recent development than royal jelly & vitamin E skin cream is the appearance on the market of complete skincare ranges containing royal jelly. By way of a warning, some of the cheap brands have minute quantities of the freeze-dried product simply so that the words 'royal jelly' can be used on the packaging.

However, there is one range in particular which uses a significant proportion of pure, fresh royal jelly. The price inevitably reflects the fresh royal jelly content, but at least you know that the products will give your skin the maximum benefits. I should state that I played a considerable part in helping to formulate the range: I knew from my own experience how beneficial royal jelly is to the skin and many of my correspondents had expressed the hope that such a range might be developed. Modern skincare formulations are more like a list of chemicals than a careful blending of natural ingredients, but this new range seems to make the most of what nature has to offer, with no animal-derived ingredients in its constituents. The range at present comprises a cleansing bar, cleansing lotion, skin tonic, moisturizer, night cream, eye gel and face mask.

Cleansing bar

This is the ideal cleanser if you prefer washing your face to using a lotion. Its balanced pH avoids the drastic changes which occur in the acid-alkali balance of your skin when you wash with soap-based cleansers. This very gentle cleansing bar contains fresh royal jelly, our old friend vitamin E, plant extracts and essential oils.

Cleansing lotion

For those who have very dry skin, the cleansing lotion is preferable. This revitalizing, light, non-greasy lotion removes all traces of make-up and grime, but at the same time gives your skin the benefits of fresh royal jelly, vitamin E, plant extracts and essential oils — a real feast for your epidermis!

Skin tonic

Toning refreshes the skin by helping to close the pores and refine the oilier areas over the forehead, nose and chin. As well as fresh royal jelly, the revitalizing skin tonic contains gammalinolenic acid-rich oil, vitamin E, menthol plant extracts, essential oils and roseflower extract. There is no alcohol in the formulation which will be a great relief to anyone with a sensitive skin.

Moisturizer

Moisturizing the skin after toning is an essential part of any skincare routine, and the light, non-clogging royal jelly moisturizer is full of good things to nourish as well as moisturize the skin. Rosehip oil, carrot oil, GLA-rich oils, soothing allantoin and beeswax combine with royal jelly and vitamin E. There is even a light sunscreen, although it is recommended that additional sunscreen be used when sunbathing.

Night cream

This is even richer and more nourishing than the moisturizer and contains the biggest percentage of royal jelly of all the products in the range. As well as essential oils, it has vitamins E and A which are both known to improve skin condition.

Eye gel

The skin around your eyes is extremely sensitive and we should be very wary about slapping on the first cream that comes to hand. However, this gel has nothing in it which could irritate or harm the delicate tissues — on the contrary, it contains royal jelly and, once again, vitamin E, as well as other natural ingredients such as soothing aloe vera.

Face mask

The best gentle but revitalizing face masks draw impurities out of the skin as well as moisturizing and nourishing it, and this one has the right mix of ingredients to carry out the task effectively. Royal jelly and vitamin E are combined with natural moisturizers in a creamy clay base and I use this excellent product regularly, once or twice a week.

These products have a natural, delicate fragrance which comes solely from the essential oils and plant extracts which have been included in the formulation because of their own intrinsic beneficial properties.

I can say with confidence that the products in this skincare range are perfectly safe for all skins, which cannot be claimed for some of the skin preparations I have used in the past. If your skin is sensitive, you will know what I mean. You will suffer from, for example, redness, blotchy patches, itchiness and rashes. It never ceases to amaze me that we are expected to pay good money for products which leave our skin in a worse state than it was before we applied them! I can vouch from my own experience for the reliability and effectiveness of these royal jelly skin products. I use them as a matter of course and my skin really feels the benefit.

All the products in the royal jelly skincare range have undergone unusually thorough and expensive testing — on people, not on animals. The night cream, which is richest in the active ingredients, was tested under full supervision on 100 volunteers, not one of whom showed an allergic or negative response. Indeed, several groups of cosmetic products were tested during that series of trials, and the fresh royal jelly range put many of the others to shame! Given the natural ingredients and absence of known allergens or irritants in these products, such a result was only to be expected.

It will be interesting to see whether these skincare products have similar effects to the royal jelly cream. There is every reason to believe they will, but it is early days yet and only time will tell.

P.S.

There is a fascinating postscript to the development of this skincare range. Vicki Dryden-Wyatt, a well-known freelance cosmetics consultant, assisted in the formulation of these products. When Vicki was first asked to work on the project she was an 'absolute cynic' about the value of fresh royal jelly. She had heard about enough 'miracle' products in her walk of life to take any claims with a very large pinch of salt. Then, on her first visit to the company, Vicki was shown their range of fresh royal jelly products and tasted a little of each, including the tonic. She left the office with samples of all the company's products, but with no change in her opinion on royal jelly.

'That night,' said Vicki, 'I didn't get home until about one o'clock in the morning. Surprisingly, I wasn't feeling at all tired, so I worked on until five o'clock. I didn't connect my newfound energy with the tonic at all.'

A few days later, Vicki had a busy evening ahead of her and decided to take a phial of the liquid royal jelly tonic before she left home, to see whether it would have any effect. 'Again, I returned home at one o'clock and worked through until dawn. It was only when I had finished work that I thought back and realized that it was thanks to the royal jelly tonic that I had felt so wide awake and full of energy on both occasions.'

Needless to say, Vicki has been taking her daily royal jelly capsule ever since, with occasional phials of tonic for extra energy. 'And I intend to carry on taking that brand of fresh royal jelly', said Vicki, firmly. 'I can definitely say that my energy levels are higher because of royal jelly. My skin, hair and nails have improved too.'

As so often happens, the royal jelly habit has spread through Vicki's family. Her husband, who is a down-to-earth farmer, decided to give the capsules a try. 'After just two weeks he noticed that he felt more energetic, too', reported Vicki. 'This may sound mad,' she went on, 'but, you know, he was bald on top and now his hair has started to grow back!'

I have so many instances of experiences like Vicki's: stories of people who begin by being totally cynical about the effects of fresh royal jelly but who, once they have tried it, become lifelong converts and fervent evangelists.

Whatever next?

It will be fascinating to see what new royal jelly products come on to the market over the next few years. If the Chinese experience is anything to go by, there is plenty of room for expansion. During my trip to China I saw a complete counter devoted to royal jelly and other bee products in the 'Friendship Shop' in Beijing. Given the fact that the East has a revered tradition of natural medicine I should not have been surprised, but some of the products left me speechless. To give just a few examples, I saw crystallized royal jelly, royal jelly chocolate, royal jelly wine — even royal jelly talcum powder!

It may be tempting to scoff at such products, but the West is only now beginning to appreciate Eastern values and Eastern wisdom in all realms of life, from abstract philosophy to practical scientific knowledge. I also feel that we, in a society dominated by materialism, junk food and the soap opera, are hardly in a position to pour scorn on beliefs and practices rooted in a respect for nature and spiritual values.

Be that as it may, whether we shall see royal jelly chocolate and wine taking the West by storm, only time will tell! Nevertheless, I am convinced that there is ample scope in the West for new royal jelly products, and I shall watch such developments with interest.

CHAPTER 4

— The Chinese connection —

Some years ago I discovered that the best royal jelly in the world comes from China and from that moment on I was determined to visit the country to see for myself how the Chinese produce such high-quality royal jelly. As soon as I began making enquiries I realized that arranging such a trip would not be without its problems. The Chinese government proved very wary about letting a Westerner observe its production methods, let alone photograph or film them, and for some time I thought I would never make the journey.

However, one day I had the idea of contacting Lord Ennals, since I knew that both he and his wife were great royal jelly enthusiasts. I therefore wrote to ask him if he would be kind enough to intercede on my behalf with the Chinese government. To my great fortune, the Labour peer was a friend of the Chinese Ambassador to the United Kingdom and, within a very short time of my request, I found that all the doors which had previously been closed to me were flung wide open. So it was that in July 1987 I became the first Westerner to witness and film the Chinese method of extracting royal jelly. Before I chronicle this fascinating trip, I should like to provide you with some background on China's position as world leader in royal jelly production and export.

Although beekeeping has a very long history, in the West it has become a booming commercial industry only over the last century. Even then, most bees are kept for their honey, rather than for the royal jelly they produce. The picture of commercial beekeeping and royal jelly production in China, however, is rather different.

There is evidence to show that the Chinese have been bee-keepers for more than 3,000 years, using their native honey bee, *Apis Cerana* (the 'wax bee'). Indeed the Chinese word for honey has been found in inscriptions on bones dating from 1400–1000 BC in the form of an ancient Chinese pictograph. Later records of honey bees can be found in the earliest collections of poetry, the *Book of Songs* (800–100 BC), and in the first etiquette manual, the

Book of Rites (100 BC). The Chinese for 'honey' and 'bee' appear in the earliest extant dictionary dating from 100 AD, and the *Book on Chinese Medicine* (*c.* 220 BC) describes honey as a very beneficial medicine. Moving on through history, medical and agricultural books written in the 11th century describe beekeeping practices in considerable detail. It seems that, at that time, bees were kept in wooden tubs and bamboo cages.

At the dawn of the 20th century, the western bee, *Apis Mellifera* (the 'honey bee'), was imported into China but still, shortly before the establishment of the People's Republic of China in 1949, there were fewer than half a million colonies and their total annual honey yield was a mere 8,000 tonnes.

With the revolution in social organization there came a revolution in Chinese attitudes to beekeeping. Less than forty years later, there are now about 6 million domesticated colonies producing more than 100,000 tonnes of honey a year. The most startling statistic, however, is that for royal jelly production — in excess of 600 tonnes annually! This figure is far ahead of any other country's output.

The reason for this 'intensive farming' of royal jelly in China is clear enough. As we saw in Chapter 3, the Chinese, more than any other race, have realized the benefits of royal jelly and use it in a very wide range of products. Indeed, less than one-third of the total Chinese royal jelly production is exported, the remainder being used in medicines and in the wide variety of royal jelly products available on the domestic market.

The importance attached to beekeeping as a whole in China is demonstrated by the fact that their Ministry of Agriculture, Animal Husbandry and Fisheries has a special department responsible for apiculture in most provinces. Its officers organize apicultural production, advise on the distribution of the various plants from which the bees extract nectar for honey-making, and they also design programmes for boosting production.

In 1958, the Institute of Apicultural Research of the Chinese Academy of Agricultural Sciences was established in Beijing. It now has a staff of 120, including 70 postgraduate researchers. The Institute plans scientific development in apiculture and co-ordinates research projects throughout the country. Some agricultural universities offer degree courses in apiculture and studies can be pursued up to doctorate level.

Given the State's wholehearted commitment to apiculture, it is hardly surprising that China has such a large output of hive products. That being said, most Chinese apiaries are small, ranging in size from 50 to 80 colonies, although at the other end of the spectrum you can find large-scale apiaries with hundreds of thousands of colonies.

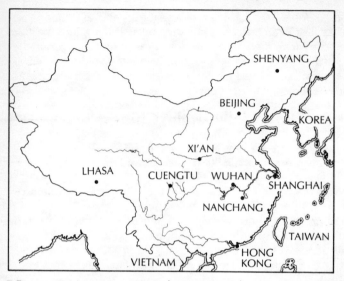

Fig 7 Fragrance Mountain is situated near Beijing, location of the Institute of Apicultural Research of the Chinese Academy of Agricultural Sciences.

On average, each beekeeper looks after 30 colonies, harvesting honey, royal jelly, pollen and propolis from his hives. In some areas, up to 2 kg of royal jelly is produced annually by each honey-bee colony.

Of course, annual yields depend not only on hive management methods, but also on the climate, and it must be remembered that China covers 9.6 million sq km, from very cold to tropical zones. Since the 1950s, to make the best of this wide range of climatic conditions, beekeepers and their colonies have migrated long distances by special trains, following the plant pollination season around the country.

The sub-tropical and tropical regions are the main areas for *Apis mellifera* colonies. The majority of these Western honey bees are the Italian strain, *Apis ligustica*, for reasons which I explained in Chapter 1. In contrast, the native Chinese bee, *Apis cerana*, can be found all over the country, particularly in the south-west and south. Over the years, these bees have adapted to the most rigorous conditions and have become very hardy.

As I have already mentioned, in earlier times Chinese bees were kept in round wooden buckets, but the annual honey yield per colony using this method was only about 5 kg per colony. As a result, movable-frame hives were introduced, increasing the yield to 15–20 kg per colony per year.

As you would expect, China produces many different kinds of honey, including jujuba, litchi, milk vetch, acacia and lime. This honey is purchased and resold by the State, most of it being supplied to medical factories and combined with Chinese herbs for the manufacture of traditional remedies. Some is also supplied to food factories for sweets, cakes and candied fruit or is bottled in food factories for sale in shops. In addition, 30,000 – 40,000 tonnes are exported annually.

——Royal jelly — the Chinese way——

During my fascinating trip to China in July 1987, I was fortunate enough to see for myself how the hives at the Fragrance Mountain Research Institute of Chinese Apiculture are managed, and how royal jelly is produced and preserved there. This beautiful corner of China is the centre of much of the world's apicultural research work, so I was able to investigate the latest developments in royal jelly production.

I have always believed that Chinese fresh royal jelly is of superior quality, and what I discovered confirmed my belief. In many other countries, beekeepers who practise intensive royal jelly production feed their bees with a sugar and water solution, and the quality of the royal jelly thus produced is markedly affected. In China, however, bees are never fed such solutions; their only source of food is the wide variety of flowering plants which abound in that country.

Fig 8 Fragrance Mountain

Fragrance Mountain is carpeted with flowers which are rich in nectar and pollen. The way these plants are cultivated is important, since there can be slight differences in the royal jelly according to the nutrition of the plants from which nectar and pollen are gathered.

The average number of bees in each of the 130 colonies at the bee farm on Fragrance Mountain is 33,000, but the structure of their hives would surprise any traditional beekeeper. Inside each hive is a specially designed frame. This frame usually supports 80 artificial 'queen cups', although it can take as many as 145. At one time, these artifical cups were made of wax, but nowadays they tend to be made of plastic. (Recent research has, in fact, proved that the amount of royal jelly collected from plastic cups exceeds that collected from the traditional beeswax versions.) The artificial queen cups hang vertically, rather than horizontally, on the frame (see Fig 9). The direction in which they lie is crucial, for in nature only cups which contain larvae destined to be queens are laid out in this configuration As a result, the worker bees are tricked into believing that they are nourishing queens and they therefore deliver royal jelly to the larvae in these cells in greater quantity and in a more concentrated form. The small worker bee larvae are gently transferred into these cups and then this section of 80 – 100 cups is attached to a frame and lowered into the hive.

Research has shown that the best time to collect royal jelly from the artificial cups is 72 hours after the frame has been introduced

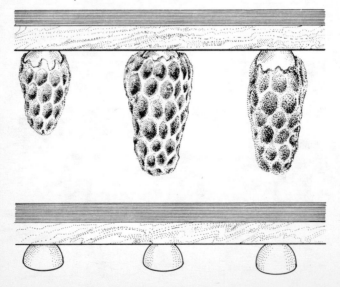

Fig 9 Artificial queen cup frame

into the hive. The Chinese have arrived at this figure for three reasons. The most important is that after three days the quality of the royal jelly is at its peak. Secondly, they have discovered that, after three days, the maximum amount of royal jelly is present in the cups. By this stage, the jelly is thicker in consistency and can no longer be ingested by the larvae. The third reason is that, as soon as the workers discover the cups, they not only begin to feed the larvae inside with royal jelly, but they also begin to deposit wax on the rim of the cups. Within five days the cups will be completely sealed and, less than a week later, the new queens will have emerged.

So, three days after the introduction of the frame, the staff of the Research Institute's bee farm remove the frame and take it indoors to cut away the beeswax deposits. Then the larvae are taken out of their royal jelly beds. Finally, the royal jelly is collected from the cups by syphoning it through a filter into a special bottle. Each cup can be expected to yield 0.3 g of royal jelly. Once the bottle is full, it is sealed and refrigerated to ensure that its contents are kept fresh and do not deteriorate. The production process then starts all over again. New larvae are introduced into the artificial queen cups before the frame is replaced in the hive.

The Chinese obtain a phenomenal success rate using this method: on the frame I inspected, 76 of the 80 queen cups contained royal jelly, so the worker bees really do think that they are feeding queens! (At this point I must stress that at no stage in the entire process are the bees harmed in any way.)

The highest annual production from any one bee colony using artificial queen frames is 2 kg per year. However, this applies only to southern China where there is a long harvesting season. In the colder northern part of the country, the royal jelly production season is restricted by the climate to May – August, so output is considerably reduced, to approximately 0.5 kg per colony.

Breeding 'super bees'

One of the many other fascinating areas of research work at Fragrance Mountain is the selective bee-breeding programme, designed to meet the increasingly large demand for royal jelly and other bee products.

I felt very honoured in being allowed to watch the workings of this programme in another research block on Fragrance Mountain. Here the researchers were hard at work breeding queen bees to develop a strain which will produce only the best royal jelly. The basis for this research is the Italian bee, which has proved such a friend to honey and royal jelly producers around the world.

The initial phase of the breeding cycle involves selecting individual drones to fertilize the queens. A great deal of 'in-breeding' goes on, since the drones are usually the offspring of the queens they will inseminate: this has been shown to improve the quality of the eventual bee products. All the bees used in the programme are from the Italian strain, both because they produce a better quality of royal jelly and because they are less likely to sting the researchers! The process of collecting donor sperm from the drones is an extremely delicate one requiring the latest microsurgery techniques.

Once the sperm has been collected, the task of artificially inseminating the queen is begun. She is sedated (with no harmful after-effects, I hasten to add) and is then inserted gently into the neck of a small tube, which holds her immobile. The sperm is then introduced into the queen bee, and the larvae which emerge from her eggs are later placed in special queen cells.

The breeding programme uses the same artificial queen cells which are used in royal jelly production, but in this case only 40 cups are used on each frame and the larvae are left alone in the hives until they hatch into queens.

It is only by close observation of the offspring of the new queen bee, examining the quality and quantity of the royal jelly produced by her worker bee children, that researchers can evaluate the success of their work. Consequently, improving the strain is a slow, laborious task, but the Chinese have great hope for the future and, fortunately, they are a very patient people!

CHAPTER 5

Fresh or freeze-dried: what's the difference?

During my Chinese trip I was particularly interested in the methods they use to preserve royal jelly. As you will have gathered by now, I firmly believe that fresh royal jelly, properly preserved, is infinitely preferable to the freeze-dried variety. It was therefore with great satisfaction that I learned from my hosts on Fragrance Mountain that royal jelly produced on the bee farm is refrigerated.

In that part of China the daytime temperature regularly rises to 30°C (86°F) and often higher. In such conditions, royal jelly is unlikely to survive outside the hive for more than a day without spoiling. I was therefore curious to know how royal jelly was preserved by those Chinese who did not own refrigerators. It transpired that many people in that country preserve their fresh royal jelly by plunging it in cold water or burying it in the earth (see Fig 10) to keep its temperature down to approximately 12°C (52°F). Even this is not quite cool enough, and the royal jelly has to be consumed within three days.

The optimum storage temperature for fresh royal jelly, in the opinion of my Chinese hosts who are the acknowledged experts, is between 5°C (41°F) and −5°C (23°F) which accords with my experience. Interestingly, they also accept storage of royal jelly at −15°C (5°F) if it has to be kept for a long time. This, of course, is well below the temperature at which royal jelly freezes, but it should be stressed that the Chinese do *not* recommend freeze-drying royal jelly, a process which both removes all the moisture content and affects the chemical structure of the substance. None of the elements is actually lost, but the molecules which make up the substance become rearranged to form new structures. The most important alteration during this process is the degradation of the amino acids, and you will have gathered from Chapter 2 that these acids are vital to royal jelly's performance in many areas.

Many people have told me that they, too, believe from their own experience that fresh royal jelly is infinitely superior to the freeze-dried variety. For instance, Katie Boyle says, 'I have tried both, and

Fig 10 Burying royal jelly in the earth

I'm sure that the dried variety is less effective than the fresh.'
Another user of fresh royal jelly told me, 'It is certainly far more
effective than any of the freeze-dried royal jellies I have used
before.'

When royal jelly products first appeared on the Western market,
they were all freeze-dried. This was mainly because no one thought
it possible to find a way of preserving royal jelly long enough for it to
be shipped, stored in warehouses and then kept on shop shelves
without freeze-drying it. Eventually a solution *was* found. It involved preserving the fresh royal jelly in honey and wheatgerm oil,
then encapsulating it in gelatin. The resulting capsules had a shelf
life of three years which is more than adequate. Incidentally, during
the search for an efficient preservative, vegetable oil was tested but
found inferior to wheatgerm oil. I would therefore advise anyone

wanting to obtain the best royal jelly capsules to look closely at the labels before deciding which brand to buy and to eschew any which contain vegetable oil rather than honey and wheatgerm oil as a preservative.

Developing a process to bring fresh royal jelly to the consumer in exactly the form in which it was taken from the hive was a long, painstaking task and many people may wonder whether it was worth the effort and the expense. Are we perhaps obsessed with the idea that the words 'pure', 'fresh', 'natural' or 'unprocessed' must mean that the product they describe is actually better than its processed equivalent?

Of course, freeze-drying (or lyophilization, as it is technically called) is a simple way of preserving royal jelly for long periods and, because of this, you will find that freeze-dried royal jelly is considerably cheaper than the fresh, but unfortunately it does seem to be much less potent. When you think about other examples of freeze-drying, this deterioration is not surprising. For instance, I defy anyone to state in all sincerity that freeze-dried coffee has exactly the same flavour as freshly ground coffee.

Even in the earliest days of my involvement with royal jelly I was convinced that the fresh product was vastly superior. However, convictions which are based on opinion rather than fact carry very little weight, so I decided to investigate the scientific literature. Relatively early on in my search I came across a fascinating paper written by scientists from the Department of Agriculture at the University of Bologna. Their work revealed that two elements in fresh royal jelly are degraded in the freeze-drying process, the sugars and the amino acids. The result of degrading the sugars is an alteration in flavour (detectable as a slightly 'roasted' taste). Although the degradation of amino acids cannot be identified by taste it seemed to me to be a disastrous side-effect of the lyophilization process. I decided to investigate further.

A Polish paper, dauntingly titled '*Amino acid composition of hydrolyzates of fresh and lyophilized royal jelly,*' shed more light on the subject. It states that 'there were significant differences between fresh and lyophilized royal jelly in the contents of lysine, serine, alanine and isoleucine (*all amino acids*), and also of sugar.'

The Poles' analysis revealed a significant reduction in the quantity of isoleucine present in the lyophilized royal jelly, but an increase in the lysine, serine and alanine content (along with a virtual 100 per cent increase in the sugar content!). Now serine and alanine can be manufactured by the body, but we have to synthesize isoleucine and lysine from the food we eat. Of all the amino acids in royal jelly, aspartic acid (which our bodies can manufacture) is present in the greatest quantity, with isoleucine coming a close second. Perhaps it is this significantly greater amount of isoleucine which accounts for the superiority of fresh over freeze-dried royal jelly. As yet, no firm conclusions have been reached.

However, during my research I came across some fascinating work carried out in the late 1970s in Egypt. In their paper, '*Royal Jelly — a Revelation or a Fable?*', which appeared in the *Egyptian Journal of Veterinary Science*, Salama, Mogawar and El-Tohamy experimented with the comparative effect of fresh and freeze-dried royal jelly on immature rats. Here, at last, was some scientific research which bore directly on my quest!

Before I go any further, I should like to reassure those readers who might disagree with experimenting on animals. As you will have gathered by now, royal jelly has no toxic effects whatsoever — after all, it is a wholly natural food.

The results of the Egyptian experiments were startling, to say the least. There were 210 female immature rats in the trial. These were divided into seven groups of 30 receiving the following quantities of royal jelly daily for four weeks.

Group 1   10 mg fresh royal jelly
Group 2   20 mg fresh royal jelly
Group 3   40 mg fresh royal jelly

Group 4   10 mg freeze-dried royal jelly
Group 5   20 mg freeze-dried royal jelly
Group 6   40 mg freeze-dried royal jelly

Group 7   0.5 ml distilled water.
(control group)

Every daily dose of royal jelly was diluted in 0.5 ml distilled water to make sure that any effects observed were not produced by the water rather than the royal jelly!

The rats were weighed each week and, in the third week, they were taken to fertile rats by night and returned to their special cages by day until the end of the experiment.

Later on, when it was obvious that a female was pregnant, she was isolated until she gave birth. The pups were counted when they were born and the scientists calculated the date of fertilization by counting back from the date of birth.

At the beginning of the experiment, the rats all weighed within 1 g of 37 g. At the end of the experiment, the average weight of each group was as follows:

Group 1   64.1 g
Group 2   74.4 g
Group 3   78.8 g

Group 4   59.0 g
Group 5   65.9 g
Group 6   71.4 g

Group 7   59.7 g.

The figures speak for themselves don't they? Simply compare those for Group 3 (40 mg fresh royal jelly), Group 6 (40 mg freeze-dried royal jelly) and Group 7 (the control group, taking distilled water only). After just four weeks, the rats fed on fresh royal jelly had streaked ahead not only of those given distilled water, but also of those given freeze-dried royal jelly! What is more, the figures for weekly growth reflect the same trend. These figures are easier to absorb when they are converted into chart form (see Fig 11).

As the Egyptian scientists themselves conclude, 'Fresh royal jelly is more potent than the lyophilized material dispensed to commerce, a fact which indicates that the process of preservation and lyophilization affected in some way the activity and potency of the material.'

But there was more to come. 'Concerning maturity, the results were very amazing: considering that the date of successful fertilization is the actual time of maturity, the results show that Group 3 (40 mg fresh royal jelly) reached maturity 26 days from the beginning of treatment — 16 days earlier than the control group. The date of maturity was related to the dose administered and the growth rate' (see Fig 12).

Even those rats given just 10 mg per day of fresh royal jelly matured 4 days before the control group, whereas those given 40 mg of freeze-dried royal jelly matured only 12 days before the control group, compared with 26 days of the 40 mg fresh royal jelly group. This effect is demonstrated clearly in the bar chart.

The scientists did point out that this early maturity might have been due to a general improvement in the condition of the rats through taking royal jelly, rather than to any direct effect which royal jelly may have on maturity, but they conceded that, whatever the case, the resulting effects were the same!

Perhaps you are wondering whether giving fresh royal jelly to your children will result in their putting on weight and reaching puberty well before they reach their teens. I can put your mind to rest on both scores.

To begin with, we have to bear in mind that the recommended adult daily dose of fresh royal jelly is 150 mg. This may well be almost four times the maximum dose given to the immature rats, but compare body weights! If a 40 kg youngster were to take the equivalent of a 40 mg dose for a 40 g rat, he would have to take 4 kg of royal jelly per day, and that would be 26,666 150 mg capsules!

Royal Jelly

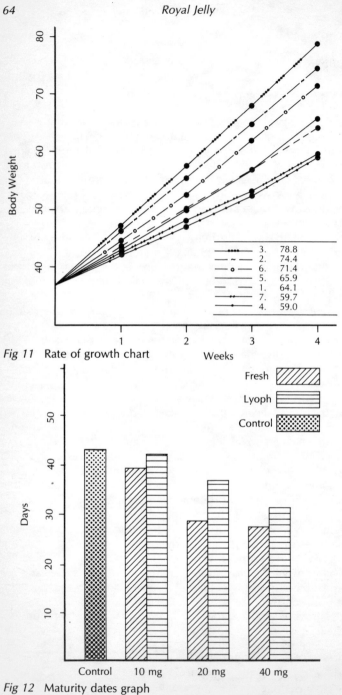

	3.	78.8
	2.	74.4
	6.	71.4
	5.	65.9
	1.	64.1
	7.	59.7
	4.	59.0

Body Weight

Weeks

Fig 11 Rate of growth chart

Fresh
Lyoph
Control

Days

Control   10 mg   20 mg   40 mg

Fig 12 Maturity dates graph

Analysis of royal jelly products using Kirlian photography techniques.

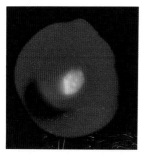

1. See how the energy radiates out. This is called, in Kirlian terms, 'the globule effect'. The mass of red colour indicates energy which is in a readily available form.

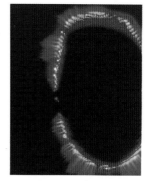

2. A fingertip before applying royal jelly and Vitamin E — the normal human aura.

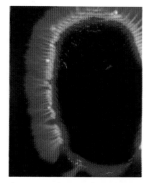

3. A fingertip after applying the cream — note the extra energy given off. This is indicated by the greater regularity and intensity of the white lines.

4. Energy radiated by a freeze-dried capsule, and a capsule which purports to contain fresh royal jelly and vegetable oil.

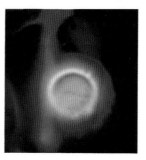

5. Energy shown to radiate from a fresh royal jelly capsule.

Mrs Thatcher, the British Prime Minister, being presented with a range of royal jelly products by the author.

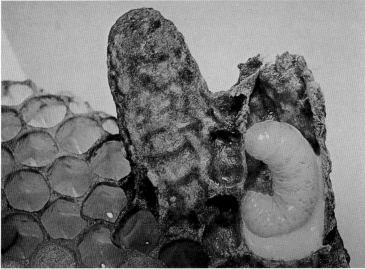

Top: A queen bee emerging from the cell.

Middle: A queen cell with royal jelly.

Right: A research worker at Fragrance Mountain placing larvae in cells.

The author's mother — Sophie Baigler (aged 79).
Opposite: Cliff Richard
Irene Stein and her two daughters, Lisa and Jane.
(Photo: Steven Hampshire)